Famous Artists
MATISSE

This edition published in 2001.

The works of Henri Matisse: © Succession H Matisse/DACS 1995

Designed and produced by
Aladdin Books Ltd
28 Percy Street
London W1P 0LD

First published in
Great Britain in 1995 by
Aladdin/Watts
96 Leonard Street
London EC2A 4XD

ISBN 0 7496 4327 7

© Aladdin Books Ltd 1995

A CIP catalogue record for this book is available from the
British Library.

Printed in UAE

Designer	Tessa Barwick
Editor	Sarah Levete
Picture research	Brooks Krikler Research
Illustrators	Michaela Stewart
	Tessa Barwick

The author, Antony Mason, is a freelance editor and author of
many books for children.

Famous Artists

MATISSE

ANTONY MASON

ALADDIN/ WATTS
LONDON • SYDNEY

Contents

The Sorrows of the King, a collage of cut and painted paper, 1952

Introduction

Henri Matisse (1869-1954) is considered to be one of the greatest and most inventive artists of the 20th century. For a time, he was at the forefront of a group of artists known as the "Fauves", whose paintings were renowned for their bold and unusual use of colour. Matisse worked hard to achieve the sense of movement and simplicity of design for which his paintings, sculptures and book illustrations became famous. Even in old age, Matisse created some of his most imaginative works, using sheets of cut paper. This book explores Matisse's development, from his discovery of painting and his training in Paris, to his final years in the south of France. The techniques he used are also discussed, and you can try some of them for yourself. Below you can see how the book is organised.

Illustration of the artist's home or environment

About the artist's work at the time

The story of the artist's life

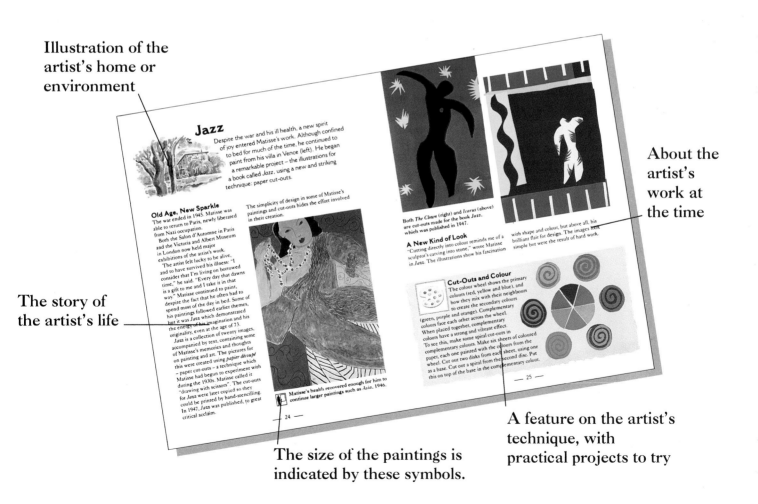

A feature on the artist's technique, with practical projects to try

The size of the paintings is indicated by these symbols.

Discovering Art

As a young man, Matisse trained to be a lawyer. It was only at the age of 20, when he was recovering from appendicitis, that he realised that the pastime of painting was to become his passion in life. In 1891, Matisse abandoned his career in law, and went to study painting and drawing in Paris (left), the art capital of the world.

An Ordinary Childhood

Henri Matisse was born on 31 December 1869 at his grandfather's house in Le Cateau-Cambrésis, a small town in northern France. His father was a grain merchant, and his mother was a hat-maker. At the age of 17, Matisse studied law in Paris, returning to his home town, Bohain, to work as a lawyer's clerk. He found the work dull, and to relieve the boredom he took art classes. In 1890, when he was confined to bed by illness, his mother gave him a set of paints. For the first time, Matisse took painting seriously.

 Still Life after de Heem's Dessert, 1893, a skilful copy of a work by a 17th-century artist

Here, Matisse shows his interest in filling his composition with strong shapes. At the start of his career, he copied the techniques of early French and Dutch painters. Later, he filled his paintings with brighter colours, and he used dark colours for outlines only.

 Woman Reading, 1894, was one of the first of Matisse's works to be exhibited.

Learning the Trade

"Once bitten by the demon of painting," he later wrote, "I never wanted to give up."

In 1891, against his father's wishes, Matisse headed for Paris to begin his artistic training. Failing to secure a place at the prestigious École des Beaux-Arts, he went instead to the Académie Julian. Here, he met the painter Albert Marquet, who became a lifelong friend. The Académie was run by a respected artist called Adolphe-William Bouguereau. Although Matisse appreciated learning the traditional skills of drawing from Bouguereau, he felt restricted by his old-fashioned approach.

At the age of 23, Matisse decided to join the more lively studio run by Gustave Moreau, a well-known painter. He encouraged Matisse to copy the work of the Old Masters in the great museums of Paris.

Still Life

A still life is a painting of everyday objects. Choose your subject – a bowl of fruit, perhaps – and decide how you want to arrange it. Do you want to include any background material to add to the image – perhaps a brightly coloured tablecloth? Study the composition, looking carefully at the texture, shape and colour of your objects. You could experiment with different styles. One version could be a detailed and realistic portrayal of the objects; another could be more abstract, conveying their shapes and colours.

A Style of his Own

At the age of 25, Matisse was at last accepted by the École des Beaux-Arts. Soon after, he got married, and had three young children to support. To make ends meet, he worked as a decorator and his wife, Amélie, worked as a milliner, making hats. Matisse's own paintings were influenced by the Impressionists, particularly in the way that he used light in his work.

A Young Family

Matisse (above) was a serious young man with a neatly trimmed beard and glasses. In 1898, he married Amélie Parayre, who adopted his four-year-old daughter, Marguerite, born to his former girlfriend Caroline Joblaud. Matisse and Amélie honeymooned in London, returning to France via Corsica. By 1900, they had two sons, Jean and Pierre. After Gustave Moreau's death in 1898, Matisse had set up his own studio. But still keen to learn, he took a course in sculpture.

In *Dinner Table*, 1897, Matisse focuses on the effect of light, as the Impressionists did.

The influence of other artists' styles on Matisse is evident here. He uses dabs of pure, bright colour in the background, which recall the Impressionists' painting of light. The tiny dots of colour are similar to the technique used by the Pointillists.

Orange Still Life, 1899, shows Matisse's fascination with light.

Developing his own Style

Matisse studied the work of other modern artists, exploring their techniques and styles to see how they suited his own ideas. He greatly admired the Post-Impressionist Paul Cézanne, who broke landscapes up into slabs of colour. He even sold his wedding ring to buy Cézanne's painting *The Three Bathers*.

Matisse found inspiration from his travels. The light of the Mediterranean was to be a continuing influence on his work. In 1904, an important art dealer, Ambroise Vollard, held an exhibition of Matisse's paintings in Paris.

Painting the Light

Experiment with capturing light, like the Impressionists. Work quickly, using little dashes, short brushstrokes or tiny dots of bright colour to give the impression of sparkling light, or of light dancing on water. For light areas, use bright colours – yellow, orange and white. For darker areas, put dots of darker colour – such as deep orange and red – next to each other. Try adding touches of a surprising colour, such as green. But you don't need to mix the colours. Your eyes will do the mixing for you!

The Wild Ones

By 1901, Matisse had met two young artists, André Derain and Maurice Vlaminck. He was attracted by their lively ideas about art; Vlaminck had even declared that he wanted "to burn down the Louvre". Together, the three artists headed a radical new style which became known as Fauvism.

Matisse's *Portrait of André Derain*, 1905, shows the energetic, rapid painting style for which the Fauves became famous.

A Change of Mood

For a while, Matisse and Amélie were in low spirits, struggling with money worries and health problems. In 1903, in order to help resolve their financial difficulties, the family left Paris to stay with Matisse's parents in Bohain.

But the summer of 1905 saw a change in the artist's mood. He and his family were staying in a Mediterranean fishing village called Collioure (above), near the Spanish border. Here they were joined by André Derain and Maurice Vlaminck.

When the three artists returned to Paris to take part in a major annual exhibition of new art, the Salon d'Automne, their work caused a sensation. Nothing like this had been seen before. The paintings were colourful, vigorous and bold. The critic Louis Vauxcelles thought it looked like the work of *fauves* (wild beasts). The painters rather enjoyed this description, and adopted the name. From 1905 to 1908, Fauvism dominated the modern art scene in Europe, before being overshadowed by a new movement, Cubism.

Throughout his life, Matisse never felt tied down to one particular style; he was always open to new ideas. In 1906, when he made his first trip to North Africa, the artist was already beginning to look for sources of inspiration that would lead him away from the wildness of the Fauves.

A Blaze of Colour

Fauvism was a movement of a loosely knit group of like-minded artists who rejected the subtle and delicate style of the Impressionists. The Fauves made little attempt to represent landscapes and people as they really appeared. Instead, they played around with the way that we see the world. They used bright, bold colours and shapes, applied in sharp brushstrokes. Perspective was not important, and their images often looked like flat surfaces.

Matisse was more concerned with the colour and design of the landscape than in copying exactly how it looked. In the style of the Fauves, he freely applies paint, creating unusual and striking combinations of primary and secondary colours (see page 25).

 The Open Window, painted in 1905, shows how the Fauves used bold and surprising colours, applied to the canvas in strong brushstrokes.

Instant Fauvism

Become a Fauve! Fold a piece of paper in half so that you have a dividing line down the middle. Choose a simple subject such as a tree; draw it in the centre of the page, so that the middle of the page divides your subject in two. Paint one side of it with realistic colours. Paint the other side in the Fauvist style, with crude, thick outlines in unexpected colours. Experiment with different combinations of colour. What is the effect of using complementary colours (see page 25) next to each other?

New Directions

Matisse's travels through Europe, Africa and the islands of the South Pacific awakened his interest in different styles and forms. Although he had left behind the dramatic style of Fauvism, Matisse's innovative work continued to cause controversy. Despite this, at the age of 39, Matisse was recognised as an outstanding artist.

Teacher and Leader

Now a successful artist whose work was exhibited in Berlin, New York, Stockholm, Moscow and London, Matisse set up his own private painting academy in Paris in 1908. This was attended by young artists from all over Europe. But three years later, Matisse decided to close the school so that he could concentrate on his own paintings.

In 1909, Matisse's family moved from Paris to a larger house and studio in a suburb of Paris called Issy-les-Moulineaux. He travelled frequently to Germany and Spain (above left), to study work by Islamic artists of the past, which he admired for its subtle patterns and colours. He filled the family home with the textiles and ceramics he had collected on his travels.

Standing Nude, pen and ink drawing, 1907–8

Matisse was fascinated by sculpture from other cultures, such as Africa and the South Pacific, admiring its strong, expressive shapes. During his lifetime, he made about 70 sculptures. He also began to look at ways of presenting scenes as flat images, filled with the colours and patterns of a scene, but without the "wild" strokes of Fauvism.

It was a difficult time for Matisse. His father died in 1910 and some of his new work, such as *Dance II* (see page 19), was much criticised. Even some of his supporters had doubts about buying his controversial work.

However, undeterred, Matisse continued to create images of calm and beauty.

Two Women is a small bronze sculpture created by Matisse in 1907.

Colour is more important here than the representation of a realistic image. Compare this to Matisse's treatment of a similar theme in *Dinner Table*, on page 8. Here, the wall and table are covered in the same pattern.

In *Harmony in Red*, 1908, flat areas of colour dominate the image.

Painting Flat

Early Renaissance artists, whom Matisse had studied when he travelled to Italy in 1907 and 1908, did not know the rules of perspective. Matisse did, but he deliberately chose to ignore them. He was more interested in filling his paintings with colour rather than in creating scenes with depth. Matisse often constructed images and patterns out of pure colour. Such flat areas of paint, applied without using perspective, were later to become a feature of Matisse's innovative technique of paper cut-outs.

Out of Perspective

Objects look smaller the further away they are. Perspective gives this sense of depth to an artist's work. Lines which in real life run

parallel, appear to meet at a single point in the distance – the "vanishing point" (above).

Experiment with painting the same scene using perspective and then painting flat, without perspective (left). Notice the new and interesting shapes that you can create.

North Africa

With his school closed, Matisse was able to devote more time to his art and travels. In 1912, he began the first of two long trips to Morocco (left) which had a profound influence on his painting. Matisse's work became coloured with a new sense of light and calm. But, back in France, a new movement – Cubism – was taking the art world by storm.

Moroccan Lights

In 1908, Matisse had written that "a work of art must be harmonious in its entirety." By contrast, the work of the Cubists, led by the young and energetic Pablo Picasso, was dark and angular; images were broken up into geometrical shapes. Although they held different views about painting, Matisse and Picasso became good friends, visiting each other's studios and exchanging paintings.

From 1912 to 1913, Matisse spent much time in Morocco. He reflected the images and colours of the Moroccan landscape in his paintings. The artist was also entranced by the beauty of the south of France, where he stayed for a while with his mother who was suffering from heart trouble. But in 1913, Matisse decided to return to Paris.

In July 1914, a large retrospective exhibition of his work was held in Berlin, but Europe was on the brink of conflict. In August, war was declared and Germany invaded Belgium and France. World War I had begun.

Matisse, now 44 years old, applied to do military service but was not accepted. His health was still troublesome. He travelled back to Collioure, where he and his family remained until November 1914. Here, he met the Cubist artist Juan Gris and even adopted some of Gris' ideas. In 1917, Matisse's sons, Jean and Pierre, left to join the army. The family was growing apart. Matisse now put more and more energy into his work.

Window at Tangier, painted in 1912

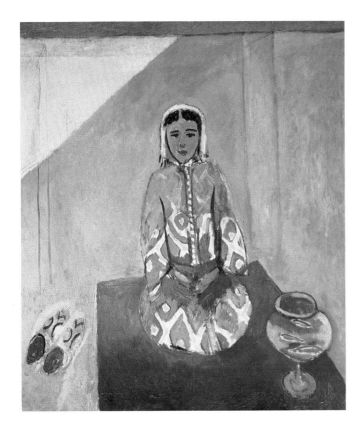

Shades of Blue and Pink

The paintings from this period show Matisse exploring shape and colour to create a mood of calm. His paintings of North Africa are very spare, with simple compositions and limited colour schemes. But he creates a sense of space and tranquillity through simple, flat areas of colour, often shades of blue and pink.

Entrance to the Kasbah, 1912 (below) is in a triptych (a set of three pictures). *Zorah on the Terrace*, 1912 (left) and *Window at Tangier*, 1912 (bottom left) complete the set, which reflects the blue light of Morocco.

Frames within Frames

Capturing images through a frame such as a window or door, helps to draw the eye through to the view. Try to paint a view through a window frame. Pencil in the outline of the window, and sketch in the details of the view. Paint the distant parts of the view with light colours. Use darker colours for objects that are nearest to you. The "vanishing point" (see page 13) will help to add depth to your scene.

Odalisques

In 1917, Matisse moved to Nice (right), a seaside town in south-eastern France. For many years after this, he divided his time between Paris and the south of France. Matisse began a series of paintings of "odalisques", which recall the exotic world of the East.

The Warmth of the South

As the war drew to a close in 1918, Matisse was living in Nice. Here he met other great artists, such as the Impressionist Auguste Renoir, who had also chosen to live in the south for its light, colour and warmth.

In 1919, Matisse went to London to create the sets and costumes for a new ballet, performed by the Ballets Russes, one of the most exciting troupes of the day. This project stimulated his interest in textile design, and, later, in paper cut-outs.

But the success of this work was also full of sorrow for Matisse. The day before the première, his mother died. Although he was now world famous, Matisse became solitary and depressed.

Odalisque with Red Trousers, 1921, reflects the more relaxed mood of the post-war period.

The White Slave, 1921–22

Shapely Forms and Textiles

Literally, "odalisques" are female slaves from the Turkish harems, the luxuriously decorated rooms where the wives and mistresses of rich men lived.

However, Matisse was more interested in creating a mood rather than in showing highly realistic images of women. His "odalisques" evoke an oriental atmosphere of calm and sleepy beauty. The women recline on couches, surrounded by beautiful textiles. Matisse creates a richness by focusing on the colours and patterns of the materials. The backgrounds are as important as the figures, but here Matisse has returned to a more traditional style of painting. The figures are shaded and rounded, and there is more use of perspective.

Odalisque in Red Trousers, 1924–25

A World of Patterns

Curtains, carpets and wallpaper can provide exciting and atmospheric backgrounds to your paintings. Try not to copy them too closely – the effect is created by the colour and pattern, not by the detail. What about painting a figure completely surrounded in patterns – perhaps sitting on a couch next to some cushions, with a carpet below and wallpaper and curtains behind? Notice how folds in material change the patterns.

Dance

In 1930, Alfred Barnes, an American art collector, commissioned Matisse to paint a mural for his private foundation in Merion, in the USA. For this, Matisse returned to the theme of dance which had featured in his paintings twenty years earlier. The project was huge; it took three years to complete.

Success and Sorrow

In 1930, Matisse set off on an adventure, travelling to New York (above), San Francisco and then to the island of Tahiti. In New York, he met Alfred Barnes to discuss the details of the mural (a painting on a wall, or hung on a wall). The mural was to be installed beneath a row of arches at Barnes' gallery. The total length of the three-piece work, painted in oil on canvas, was over 12 metres. It was such a huge project that Matisse had to hire an old film studio in Nice to begin work on it.

Matisse started out with a design that was similar to *Dance II*, which he had painted in 1910. Gradually, however, the figures became bolder and more stylised. As he designed the mural, Matisse worked with huge pieces of paper and painted cut-outs. He wanted to create images that would not overshadow the other works displayed in the gallery, painted by such great artists as Cézanne and Renoir.

The commission caused considerable problems. Matisse had to abandon his original mural because the measurements that he had been sent were too small! He had to begin all over again. There was a price to pay for the eventual success of the mural. The three years of labour that the artist had devoted to them weakened his health. Matisse's relationship with his wife became increasingly strained. They now led separate lives. Matisse concentrated fully on his work – paintings, sculptures and drawings.

Dance II (above) was painted in 1910. *Dance I*, 1931–32 (below), oil on canvas, is the first version of the mural, which was made to incorrect measurements.

Figures in Motion

Make your paper move! Place three sheets of different coloured paper on top of each other. On the top sheet, draw a large, simple figure. Hold the sheets together and cut out the figure. Separate the limbs from each of the figures and arrange them on paper. You can make each one move like a puppet – try combining different colours.

Changing Times

Europe was in growing turmoil as the aggression of the Nazis in Germany pushed the world towards war. But despite this, his poor health and his recent separation from Amélie, Matisse continued to express calmness and tranquillity in his art. During the 1930s, he also began to work on designs for tapestries (left) and to illustrate books.

Endings and Beginnings

In 1937, Matisse became seriously ill and spent some time in hospital. After this, he remained in the south of France, moving to the Hotel Regina in Cimiez, high up in the hills of Nice.

Matisse now regularly painted the same model, a young and beautiful Russian woman called Lydia Delectorskaya, who had originally joined him as his secretary in 1933.

Matisse was taking a growing interest in French literature, illustrating the works of several of the great French poets. For these he produced lithographs – prints made by applying wax to stone.

Pink Nude, 1935, shows Matisse in a bolder mood than seen in the "odalisques".

Finding the Form

Matisse's portrayal of women was no longer of "odalisques", clothed in rich materials. Instead, he focused on simple and directly posed figures, often nudes. He was interested in conveying the form of the body. To create *Pink Nude* (below left), Matisse made many drawings using paper cut-outs. This helped him to achieve the final form, with its exaggerated limbs seeming to extend beyond the canvas, as in the *Dance* murals. The design of his work remained striking, with blocks of pure colour.

 The black highlights the simple but bold use of colour and shape in *Reader against a Black Background*, painted in 1939.

Everything in this painting appears flat. The face is treated like a shape. Like a cartoon sketch, it is made up of simple lines, but the simplicity conveys great depth of expression.

Outline

Strong outline can have a dramatic effect. To see this for yourself, try doing two paintings of a similar subject. Draw the outlines for both in pencil. In the first painting, take the colour up to the pencil outlines. Use gentle shading to show any shape or shadow, and the rounded forms of the objects. Fill the whole picture with colour. In the second version, paint in the main outlines in thick brushstrokes, using dark colours such as black, brown or deep mauve. Work quickly, so the outlines are bold and smooth. When the outlines are dry, fill them with colour. Which do you prefer?

World War II

In September 1939, war was declared. Matisse decided to spend the war years in southern France. At the age of 71, he had a major operation for cancer. The artist came close to death, but made a remarkable recovery. In 1943, after an air raid on the Hotel Regina in Cimiez, Matisse (left) moved to Vence, a small town in the nearby hills.

The War Years

Matisse could have left France at the start of the war, but he chose to remain in Nice. This became a part of Vichy France, an area ruled by French politicians who had made a treaty with the Nazi Germans. In 1944, Amélie and Marguerite, Matisse's ex-wife and daughter, were arrested (and later released) by the Gestapo, the Nazi police, for their activities in the resistance – the movement against the German occupation in France.

The Conversation, 1941, shows a recurrent theme in Matisse's work – two people talking.

Simplicity and Calm

During the war, artists' materials were in short supply, but Matisse continued his busy life of painting and drawing. His work shows little of the strain of war. He remained true to his desire to paint pictures of calm and tranquillity. In 1908, he had written: "What I dream of is an art of balance, of purity and serenity, free of any troubling subject matter."

In this period, the women Matisse painted were often clothed in blouses and evening gowns, wearing strings of pearls, seated in their living rooms, set against rich backgrounds. But in *The Rumanian Blouse*, Matisse reverses this style. Here it is not the background pattern which dominates, but the embroidery on the blouse itself. Matisse used the pattern on the blouse in several other paintings.

The Rumanian Blouse is a portrait of Lydia, painted in 1940.

There is always an element of surprise in Matisse's compositions. The background to *The Conversation* is split into two large areas of colour, which adds to the sense of a two-sided conversation. The background does not quite touch the outline of the face, creating a softening effect.

Self Portraits

In portraits, Matisse used bold outlines and simple lines to show facial features. To draw a picture of yourself, try sitting in front of a mirror. Work quickly to create a sense of yourself, rather than concentrating on the detail. What is the effect if you work without looking at your piece of paper?

Jazz

Despite the war and his ill health, a new spirit of joy entered Matisse's work. Although confined to bed for much of the time, he continued to paint from his villa in Vence (left). He began a remarkable project – the illustrations for a book called *Jazz*, using a new and striking technique: paper cut-outs.

Old Age, New Sparkle

The war ended in 1945. Matisse was able to return to Paris, newly liberated from Nazi occupation.

Both the Salon d'Automne in Paris and the Victoria and Albert Museum in London now held major exhibitions of the artist's work.

The artist felt lucky to be alive, and to have survived his illness: "I consider that I'm living on borrowed time," he said. "Every day that dawns is a gift to me and I take it in that way." Matisse continued to paint, despite the fact that he often had to spend most of the day in bed. Some of his paintings followed earlier themes, but it was *Jazz* which demonstrated the energy of his imagination and his originality, even at the age of 73.

Jazz is a collection of twenty images, accompanied by text, containing some of Matisse's memories and thoughts on painting and art. The pictures for this were created using *papier découpé* – paper cut-outs – a technique which Matisse had begun to experiment with during the 1930s. Matisse called it "drawing with scissors". The cut-outs for *Jazz* were later copied so they could be printed by hand-stencilling. In 1947, *Jazz* was published, to great critical acclaim.

The simplicity of design in some of Matisse's paintings and cut-outs hides the effort involved in their creation.

 Matisse's health recovered enough for him to continue larger paintings such as *Asia*, 1946.

Both *The Clown* (right) and *Icarus* (above) are cut-outs made for the book *Jazz*, which was published in 1947.

A New Kind of Look

"Cutting directly into colour reminds me of a sculptor's carving into stone," wrote Matisse in *Jazz*. The illustrations show his fascination with shape and colour, but above all, his brilliant flair for design. The images look simple but were the result of hard work.

Cut-Outs and Colour

The colour wheel shows the primary colours (red, yellow and blue), and how they mix with their neighbours to create the secondary colours (green, purple and orange). Complementary colours face each other across the wheel. When placed together, complementary colours have a strong and vibrant effect. To see this, make some spiral cut-outs in complementary colours. Make six sheets of coloured paper, each one painted with the colours from the wheel. Cut out two discs from each sheet, using one as a base. Cut out a spiral from the second disc. Put this on top of the base in the complementary colour.

The Vence Chapel

Matisse had been nursed through his illness by a Dominican nun called Sister Jacques. In 1948, she asked if he would be interested in designing some stained-glass windows for a new chapel in Vence. Matisse gladly accepted the challenge. Although he was bedridden for much of the time (left), he continued to create masterpieces.

A New Lease of Life

Now aged nearly 80, the artist was determined to continue working. Matisse found that he could design and paint from his bed by using a brush attached to a bamboo pole.

The end of World War II saw many artists turn their attention to religious themes, as if they wanted to find some meaning in life after the devastation and destruction of the war years. Although he was not a follower of any particular faith, Matisse had always felt that his art was in some way an expression of a religious feeling. In 1948, Matisse contributed paintings to a new church called Notre-Dame-de-Toute-Grâce, at Assy. That same year, at the request of Sister Jacques, he began work on the chapel at Vence.

But Matisse did not simply work on the stained glass – he took over the entire decoration of the chapel, designing the murals and even the priest's robes and the crucifix. He felt that "this is essentially a work of art...The essential thing is to put oneself in a frame of mind which is close to that of prayer." Matisse was delighted with the result of his work on the chapel, saying "I consider it my masterpiece."

Large Red Interior was painted in 1948.

Matisse kept the designs very simple – black lines against white. Later these images were transferred in black enamel paint onto white ceramic tiles. Light is reflected from the cut-out patterns of the stained glass.

The altar and mural at the Chapel of the Rosary in Vence

Painting with Light

The essential colour of the interior of the Matisse chapel is white; during the daytime the floor and walls become dappled with the soft, coloured light cast by the stained glass. Simplicity and spontaneity were always strong features of Matisse's paintings. In 1948, he wrote: "I have always...wished my works to have the lightness and joyousness of springtime which never lets anyone suspect the labours it has cost."

Murals

Have a go at designing a mural – but you don't need to paint the wall! Like Matisse, you can design a mural on paper. Use the largest sheet of paper that you can find – perhaps the back of a left-over roll of wallpaper. Pin this to the wall. Create a large, bold pattern with a strong and simple design. Try tying your paintbrush to a long stick. It may be hard to control at first, and you may need to practise, but it will help you to work on a large scale.

Spirit in Old Age

Although Matisse's failing health prevented him from doing much painting, he continued to work energetically. In his old age, Matisse produced some of the best and most inventive work of his life. He concentrated on large-scale paper cut-outs, which provided him with a new and exciting form of expression.

Genius to the Last

In 1949, Matisse moved back to the Hotel Regina in Cimiez, where he was to spend most of the rest of his life. Soon the walls of his studio were covered with cut-outs. Matisse suffered increasingly from asthma and heart trouble. Cut-outs provided a way for him to continue working when his health prevented him from standing at an easel and painting. But the cut-outs did not simply replace painting: they were themselves a new and important art form. He would do the cut-outs himself, and then from his wheelchair (above), he would direct Lydia to position the pieces on backgrounds pinned to the wall.

In 1950, he was awarded the Grand Prix at the Venice Biennale, one of the largest festivals of modern art in the world. It was a great tribute to an artist who was now 81 years old – but in fact Matisse's new work showed the youthful vigour of a man a quarter of his age.

Matisse was a kindly old man, humble about his achievements. He remained open to fresh ideas and followed developments in modern art. When he saw the new and very free abstract work by younger artists, he said that he did not understand it, and so would not judge it!

In 1952, he helped to found the Musée Matisse in his birthplace, Le Cateau-Cambrésis. Matisse's last work dates from 1953, when he was 84. He died at Cimiez the following year, on 3 November 1954.

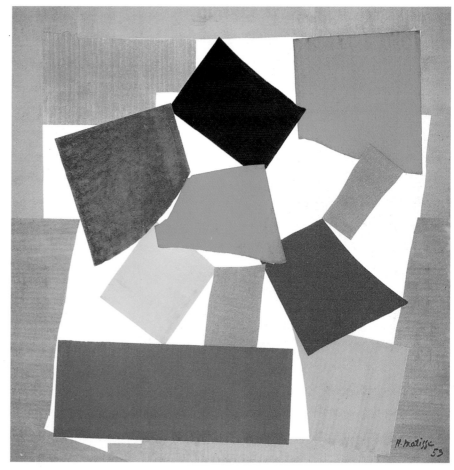

The Snail, a painted paper cut-out created in 1953, is one of Matisse's last works.

Blue Nude IV, 1952, is in a series of
blue cut-outs of nudes and dancers.

Colour and Shape

Some of Matisse's last cut-outs are
acknowledged as his greatest
masterpieces. They show his experience
in composition, and his combination
of colours. Some of these works are
abstract – they consist of shapes, rather
than recognisable images of the real
world. Nonetheless, Matisse gave
them names, such as *The Snail*, which tie
them to things seen in the real world.

The foot of the *Blue Nude* is simplified
to just three toes. Every part of the image
is essential: nothing could be added or
taken away without spoiling the effect.

Paper Cut-Outs

Paper cut-outs make bold,
strong images. They are
composed of flat areas of
colour, so the designs have
to be simple to be effective. Try making
a cut-out with only a few different shapes.
This cut-out picture (right) is made up
mainly from circles and petal shapes.
Use printed coloured paper, or select your
own colour range by painting sheets of
paper with the colours that you want to use
– make sure the paint is dry before you start
cutting the shapes! Put a few sheets on top
of each other to cut out lots of shapes.

Chronology of Matisse's Life

1869 Born on 31 December in France.

1888 Began work as a lawyer's clerk.

1891 Began art training in Paris.

1894 Marguerite born to Caroline Joblaud.

1895 Accepted by the École des Beaux Arts, Paris.

1898 Married Amélie Parayre, who happily adopted Marguerite.

1899 Birth of their first son, Jean.

1900 Birth of their second son, Pierre.

1901 Matisse met André Derain and Maurice Vlaminck.

1904 Exhibition at Ambroise Vollard gallery in Paris.

1905 Fauvism was given its name.

1906 First visit to North Africa. Met Picasso.

1908 The end of Fauvism

1912–13 Made two important trips to Morocco.

1925 Awarded Legion of Honour by the French government.

1927 Matisse awarded First Prize at the Carnegie International Exhibition in Nice.

1930–33 Painted *Dance* murals.

1939 Settled in Nice during World War II.

1941 Matisse came close to death. He never fully recovered.

1947 Publication of *Jazz*

1950 Awarded the Grand Prix at the Venice Biennale.

1951 Completion of the chapel in Vence.

1954 Matisse died on 3 November at Cimiez, Nice, from a heart attack.

A Brief History Of Art

The world's earliest works of art are figurines dating from 30,000 BC. Cave art developed from 16,000 BC. In the Classical Age (500–400 BC) sculpture flourished in Ancient Greece.

The Renaissance period began in Italy in the 1300s and reached its height in the 16th century. Famous Italian artists include Giotto (c1266–1337), Leonardo da Vinci (1452–1519), Michelangelo Buonarroti (1475–1564) and Titian (c1487–1576).

In Europe during the 15th and 16th centuries, Hieronymus Bosch (active 1480–1516), Albrecht Dürer (1471–1528), Pieter Breughel the Elder (1525–69) and El Greco (1541–1614) produced great art. Artists of the Baroque period include Peter Paul Rubens (1577–1640) and Rembrandt van Rijn (1606–69).

During the Romantic movement, English artists JMW Turner (1775–1851) and John Constable (1776–1837) produced wonderful landscapes. Francisco Goya (1746–1828) was a great Spanish portrait artist.

Impressionism began in France in the 1870s. Artists include Claude Monet (1840–1926), Camille Pissarro (1830–1903) and Edgar Degas (1834–1917). Post-Impressionists include Paul Cézanne (1839–1906), Paul Gauguin (1848–1903) and Vincent van Gogh (1853–90).

The 20th century saw many movements in art. Georges Braque (1882–1963) painted in the Cubist tradition, Salvador Dalí (1904–89) in the Surrealist. Pablo Picasso (1881–1973) was a prolific Spanish painter. More recently, Jackson Pollock (1912–56) and David Hockney (1937) have achieved fame.

Museums & Galleries

The museums and galleries listed below have examples of Matisse's work:

Musée Matisse, Nice, France

Musée Matisse, Le Cateau-Cambrésis, France

Musée National d'Art Moderne, Centre Georges Pompidou, Paris, France

Musée d'Art Moderne de la Ville de Paris, France

Musée de Peinture et de Sculpture, Grenoble, France

Tate Modern, London, England

Museum of Modern Art, New York, USA

Museum of Fine Arts, Boston, USA

Art Institute of Chicago, USA

Baltimore Museum of Art, Maryland, USA

Barnes Foundation, Merion, USA

Philadelphia Museum of Art, USA

National Gallery of Canada, Ottawa, Canada

Neue Pinakothek, Munich, Germany

Staatsgalerie, Stuttgart, Germany

Statens Museum for Kunst, Copenhagen, Denmark

Pushkin Museum, Moscow, Russia

The Hermitage Museum, St Petersburg, Russia

Glossary

Abstract art Paintings which consist entirely of patterns and shapes, and do not attempt to portray anything in the real world.

Complementary colours A system which divides contrasting colours into opposites, as shown by the colour wheel. Each primary colour has an opposing secondary colour.

Cubism An art movement, dating from 1907, in which paintings and sculptures are broken up into geometric forms and shapes.

Fauve This name, relating to the French word for a wild animal, was given to a loose-knit group of artists who painted in vivid colours in about 1905–8. **Matisse** was considered to be the leader of the Fauves.

Flat In painting, "flat" refers to an area covered by a single, plain colour, without shading or varying tones which might give the illusion of depth.

Impressionism The name given in the 1870s to a group of artists (Monet, Renoir, Sisley, Pissarro and others) who evoked the passing mood of a landscape or scene by working rapidly, using quick brushstrokes.

Perspective Since the 15th century, artists have used perspective to suggest distance in their paintings. As a general rule, objects look smaller the further away they are.

Post-Impressionism The name given to several artists of the late 19th century whose work followed that of the Impressionists. They include Cézanne and Gauguin.

Pointillism A painting technique in which thousands of tiny dots of pure colour are used to create an image. The key Pointillists were Georges Seurat and Paul Signac.

Index

Index of Pictures